The Book of Southern Wisdom

Common Sense and Uncommon Genius
From 101 Great Southerners

Compiled and Edited by Criswell Freeman

WALNUT GROVE PRESS
Nashville, TN

ISBN 0-9640955-3-X

The ideas expressed in this book are not, in all cases, exact quotations, as some have been edited for clarity and brevity. In all cases, the author has attempted to maintain the speaker's original intent. In some cases, material for this book was obtained from secondary sources, primarily print media. While every effort was made to ensure the accuracy of these sources, the accuracy cannot be guaranteed. For additions, deletions, corrections or clarifications in future editions of this text, please write WALNUT GROVE PRESS.

Printed in the United States of America

Book Design by Armour&Armour
Cover Design by Mary Mazer

4 5 6 7 8 9 10 • 97 98 99 00 01 02 03

ACKNOWLEDGMENTS
The author gratefully acknowledges the helpful support of Angela Beasley, June Bowen, Buck Cole, Richard Courtney, Mary Jo Freeman, Maryglenn McCombs, Steve Parker, Don Pippen, Karyn Richter, Bette Schnitzer, and George Schnitzer.

To My Parents

Mary and Dick Freeman

The Two Wisest Southerners I Know

Table of Contents

Introduction

For two decades, I've collected gems of wisdom on 3x5 cards. As an avid reader of quote books, I'll let you in on a secret: good Southerner quotations are hard to find.

No longer. You now hold in your hands a collection of great sayings from notable sons and daughters of the South. Their words reveal a wisdom that is distinctly Southern, a genius that has been forged in the furnace of adversity.

I've taken certain liberties in choosing contributors for this book. Mark Twain, a Midwestern native, was included because of his extended tenure as a Mississippi river boat captain and his brief service in the Confederate militia. I also included several Texans. While Texas may qualify as a region unto itself, we Tennesseans are acutely aware of our shared Southern ties with the Lone Star State. Sam Houston, for example, was not only a lawyer in my hometown of Nashville, but also the first president of Texas. When it comes to Southern heritage, it's truly a small world.

It is important to note that this is *not* a traditional book of quotations. In some cases, I have edited text in order to improve clarity (always, of course, retaining the intent of the authors' original words). And, as a Doctor of Clinical Psychology, I have chosen thoughts that reinforce the principles of good constructive thinking.

Enjoy the distinctive genius of the South. It's a wisdom born south of the Mason-Dixon line — the profound common sense of Dixie.

1

All-Purpose Advice

Katherine Anne Porter, the Texas writer, always considered herself a citizen of the Old South. Like many of her fellow Southerners, she had valuable wisdom to share. Porter, however, did not dispense casual recommendations to others. She warned, "Never take advice, including this."

With apologies to Miss Porter, the following Southern wisdom is offered for your consideration.

Do something worth remembering.

Elvis Presley

Whenever you do a thing, act as if
all the world were watching.

Thomas Jefferson

Go very lightly on the vices.

Satchel Paige

Suffer the growing pains.

Lillian Hellman

Keep your business affairs in your own hands.
It's the only way to be happy.

Martha Washington

Do the common things of life in an uncommon way.

George Washington Carver

Don't allow the future to scare you.

Tennessee Williams

Don't hide from the past. It won't catch you —
if you don't repeat it.

Pearl Bailey

Picture in your mind a sense
of personal destiny.

Wayne Oates

Make it a point to do something every day
that you don't want to do. This is the
golden rule for acquiring the habit
of doing your duty without pain.

Mark Twain

Make hay while the sun shines.

Southern Saying

Don't let your mouth write a check
your tail can't cover.

Bo Diddley

Combine a tough mind
and a tender heart.

Martin Luther King, Jr.

Dare to risk public criticism.

Mary Kay Ash

Use your eyes as if tomorrow
you would be stricken blind.

Helen Keller

Patience will give you what you want.

Ray Charles

Each day, look for a kernel of excitement.

Barbara Jordan

Never buy what you don't want
because it is cheap.

Thomas Jefferson

Inspire children.

Hank Aaron

2

Life

A Virginian, Thomas Jefferson, observed that human beings have an innate right to "life, liberty, and the pursuit of happiness." With these words, Jefferson added his name to a long list of Southern philosophers who have commented on the human condition. Consider the following thoughts on that most precious of possessions: life.

To begin with, you must know what you want.

Mary Kay Ash

Life and living aren't the same. Life is
more than just drawing breath.

Elvis Presley

Life is either a daring adventure or nothing.
To keep your face toward change and behave
like a free spirit in the presence of fate
is strength undefeatable.

Helen Keller

Life doesn't give you all the practice races
you need.

Jesse Owens

Don't believe there's plenty of time for everything. There isn't.

Lillian Hellman

Age is a question of mind over matter.
If you don't mind, it doesn't matter.

Satchel Paige

Time can be your best friend or
your worst enemy.

Ray Charles

We cannot truly face life until we face the fact
that it will be taken away from us.

Billy Graham

Life's sand runs fast.

Sam Houston

People see God every day; they just
don't always recognize him.

Pearl Bailey

Life is an unanswered question, but let's
still believe in the dignity and
importance of the question.

Tennessee Williams

All our lives we are preparing to be something
or somebody, even if we don't know it.

Katherine Anne Porter

As human beings, we were born to improvise.
Butterfly McQueen

The idea of life is to give and receive.
Dizzy Gillespie

Play is a vital part of life.

Dinah Shore

Believe in life.

W. E. B. Du Bois

3

Hope

Tuscumbia, Alabama, native Helen Keller observed, "Nothing can be done without hope and optimism." Southerners know the value of hope. After all, on more than one occasion, it was all that remained after everything else had been taken away.

Hopeful slaves dreamed of freedom and eventually won it. The defeated South relied upon faith during the rebuilding years after the Civil War. And individuals too numerous to count have shown the same kind of faith and optimism that allowed young Helen to touch the hearts of millions. You and I can use that same brand of faith in our own struggles.

Hope

The past is dead; let it bury its dead, its hopes
and its aspirations; before you lies the future —
a future full of golden promise.

Jefferson Davis

From his last speech

While I breathe, I hope.

South Carolina State Motto

Tomorrow is ours to win or to lose.

Lyndon Baines Johnson

If you want faith, you have to work for it.

Flannery O'Connor

There is no sadder sight than a young pessimist.

Mark Twain

Keep hope alive.

Jesse Jackson

Think to yourself, "I'm going to hit the ball,"
and you can.

Ty Cobb

Many a losing entry has had every attribute
except one: the belief he was going to win.
Grantland Rice

Hope is a gift we give ourselves,
and it remains when all else is gone.
Naomi Judd

Believe you can make a difference, and you will.
Bill Clinton

A master can tell you what he expects of you.
A teacher, however, awakens
your own expectations.
Patricia Neal

Hope

Every time a child is born, regardless of the
circumstances, the potentiality of the
human race is born again.

James Agee

Humanity is just a work in progress.

Tennessee Williams

I believe that man will not merely endure.
He will prevail.

William Faulkner

This is America. We can do anything here.

Ted Turner

Keep away from people who try to belittle your ambitions.

Mark Twain

I like dreams of the future
better than history
of the past.

Thomas Jefferson

4

Adversity

Sherman's March to the Sea. The defeated Confederacy. Poverty. Slavery and segregation. Without question, the South has experienced more than its share of pain.

This sampling of common sense comes courtesy of men and women who have faced adversity, struggled, and triumphed.

Y ou'll never miss the water till the well runs dry.

W. C. Handy

U nfortunate luck —that's nothin'
to worry about.

Muddy Waters

T ake the breaks in stride.

Bobby Jones

C omfort and prosperity have never enriched
the world as much as adversity.

Billy Graham

T oo many victories weaken you. The defeated
can rise up stronger than the victor.

Muhammad Ali

I learned much more
from defeat than I ever
learned from winning.

Grantland Rice

I was *blessed* with humble beginnings.

Dolly Parton

Learn how to laugh under trying circumstances.

W. C. Handy

God doesn't believe in the easy way.

James Agee

I thank God for my handicaps, for through them
I have found myself, my work, and my God.

Helen Keller

Apparent failure often proves a blessing.

Robert E. Lee

No experience is a bad experience
	unless you gain nothing from it.
							Lyndon Baines Johnson

One problem thoroughly understood is
	of more value than a score poorly mastered.
							Booker T. Washington

Everybody must learn to lose because
you can't play the game if you can't take losing.
							Arthur Ashe

Sometimes, you have to lose before
		you can learn how to win.
							Dale Earnhardt

Winners get scars too.

							Johnny Cash

Character cannot be developed in ease and quiet. Only through experience of trial and suffering can the soul be strengthened.

Helen Keller

Trouble is a part of life, and if you don't share it, you don't give others the chance to love you enough.

Dinah Shore

Don't look forward to the day when you stop suffering. Because when it comes, you'll know that you're dead.

Tennessee Williams

Between grief and nothing, I will take grief.

William Faulkner

It is our duty to make the best of our misfortunes.

George Washington

The ultimate measure of a man is not where he stands in moments of comfort and convenience, but where he stands at times of challenge and controversy.

Martin Luther King, Jr.

On those days when you feel the worst, when you think that everything is hopeless — sometimes the best things happen.

Walker Percy

Don't give up at half time. Concentrate on winning the second half.

Bear Bryant

Defeat in this world
is no disgrace if you
fought well and fought for
the right thing.

Katherine Anne Porter

You win some, you lose some, you wreck some.

Dale Earnhardt

5

Success

Success is almost as difficult to define as it is to achieve. What follows are observations about success and failure from men and women who, because they have lived, have tasted both.

Success isn't measured by the position you reach in life; it's measured by the obstacles you overcome.

Booker T. Washington

Success, we must remember, is in the eye
of the beholder.

Tennessee Ernie Ford

Failure isn't so bad if it doesn't attack the heart.
Success is all right if it doesn't go to the head.

Grantland Rice

Success is being able to come home,
lay your head on the pillow and sleep in peace.

Herschel Walker

On the clarity of your ideas depends the scope
of your success in any endeavor.

James Robertson

Keep trying and keep hitting the ball —
you may chance upon a lucky break.

Bobby Jones

It's not enough to get all the breaks.
You've got to know how to use them.

Huey P. Long

When you make a mistake, admit it; learn from it and don't repeat it.

Bear Bryant

One important key to success is
self-confidence. An important key
to self-confidence is preparation.

Arthur Ashe

To be a great champion, believe you're the best.
If you're not, pretend you are.

Muhammad Ali

We must change in order to survive.

Pearl Bailey

You've got to continue to grow, or you're
just like last night's cornbread — stale and dry.

Loretta Lynn

I have learned one great truth. The answer
to all our problems comes to a single word.
That word is "education."

Lyndon Baines Johnson

Fight for your education.

Ty Cobb

There is no defense or security for any of us
except in the highest intelligence
and development of all.

Booker T. Washington

Ninety-nine percent of failures come from
people who have the habit of making excuses.

George Washington Carver

There is in this world no such force as
the force of a man determined to rise.

W. E. B. Du Bois

Heart is what separates the good from the great.

Michael Jordan

Do you want to be successful? Nurture your talent.

Tennessee Ernie Ford

6

Freedom

Mahatma Gandhi, the Indian proponent of non-violence, wrote, "The moment a slave resolves that he will no longer be a slave, his fetters fall." The struggle for individual freedom has crossed all national borders; it has faced every generation. History reveals that the price of liberty is often quite dear.

Freedom is sometimes purchased on the battlefield, sometimes won in the legislature, and sometimes discovered inside the human heart. Here are the words of Southerners who have fought their own battles for freedom — and seen their own fetters fall.

Liberty, when it begins to take root,
    is a plant of rapid growth.

George Washington

The human soul cannot be
    permanently chained.

W. E. B. Du Bois

The boisterous sea of liberty is
    never without a wave.

Thomas Jefferson

You have to pay a very large price for freedom.

Lillian Hellman

Freedom is not free.

Martin Luther King, Jr.

The only thing that can free you is the belief that you can be free.

Oprah Winfrey

Your struggle to be free is different from mine,
but we are kinspersons in that we both struggle.

Wayne Oates

To be free is to have achieved your life.

Tennessee Williams

We are free not because we claim freedom
but because we practice it.

William Faulkner

You can't hold a man down without
staying down with him.

Booker T. Washington

All oppressed people are authorized, whenever
they can, to rise and break their fetters.

Henry Clay

A little rebellion now and then is a good thing.

Thomas Jefferson

The highest result of education is tolerance.

Helen Keller

We have enough trouble in this old world
without hating people because of the
color of their skin.

Archie Campbell

Being distracted by the color of a
person's skin is something I just can't see.

Ray Charles

Virtue knows no color lines.

Ida B. Wells

Freedom

Injustice anywhere is a threat to justice
everywhere.

Martin Luther King, Jr.

The cost of liberty is less then the price
of repression.

W. E. B. Du Bois

I know not what course others may take, but
as for me, give me liberty or give me death.

Patrick Henry

7

Happiness

How can we achieve happiness? This simple riddle can be a knotty problem. Even when we discover answers, they can be difficult to put into practice. To complicate matters, the more we chase contentment, the more elusive it becomes.

Some helpful advice is found in the words of these Southerners. They give us valuable insight into that universal human quest — the search for happiness.

Happiness cannot come from without. It must come from within.

Helen Keller

This is happiness; to be
dissolved into something
complete and great.

Willa Cather

Keep trying to win;
keep playing the game;
but keep room in your heart
for a song.

Grantland Rice

Man's real life is happy chiefly because
he is ever expecting that it will soon be so.

Edgar Allan Poe

A man without ambition is dead. A man with
ambition but no love is dead. A man with
ambition and love for his blessings
here on earth is ever so alive.

Pearl Bailey

Grief can take care of itself, but to get the
full value of joy, you must have
somebody to divide it with.

Mark Twain

When the door of happiness closes,
another opens; but often we look so long
at the closed door that we do not see
the one that has been opened for us.

Helen Keller

It is neither wealth nor splendor, but tranquility
and occupation, which give happiness.

Thomas Jefferson

The happiest people are those who do
the most for others.

Booker T. Washington

The greater part of our happiness depends on our disposition and not our circumstances.

Martha Washington

I don't want to be a slave to my own willpower.

Will D. Campbell

8

Politics

Aristotle observed that, "Man is by nature a political animal." When it comes to politics, Southerners mix a healthy dose of party loyalty, a dash of grass roots appeal, and, in many cases, a heaping helping of conservatism.

The South has produced a string of leaders — some great, some not-so-great, some most colorful.

If you want to go into politics, first
get your name known.

Davy Crockett

The government is best which governs least.

Thomas Jefferson

More is lost by the long continuance of
men in office than is generally to be gained
by their experience.

Andrew Jackson

The passion for office among members of
Congress is very great, if not disreputable,
and greatly embarrasses the operations
of government.

James K. Polk

All men having power ought to be distrusted
to a certain degree.

James Madison

I seldom think about politics more than
18 hours a day.

Lyndon Baines Johnson

A politician ought be born a foundling and
remain a bachelor.

Lady Bird Johnson

I understand the rules of war in politics.
No one has practiced them more.

Huey P. Long

If you're in politics, and you can't tell when
you walk into a room who's for you and
who's against you, then you're
in the wrong line of work.

Lyndon Baines Johnson

In a political fight, when you've got nothing
in favor of your side, spread dissension
in the opposition camp.

Huey B. Long

There are no necessary evils in government.
Its evils exist only in its abuses.

Andrew Jackson

No nation is better that the individuals
that compose it.

Cordell Hull

If more politicians were thinking about
the next generation instead of the next election,
it would be better for the United States and
for the world.

Claude Pepper

Courts and cabinet, the President and
     his advisers derive their power and
     their greatness from the people.

Andrew Johnson

It is incumbent on each generation
     to pay its debts as it goes.

Thomas Jefferson

A national debt is a national curse.

Andrew Jackson

The stakes are too high
for government to be a
spectator sport.

Barbara Jordan

America will endure, and
the causes of human freedom
will triumph.

Cordell Hull

9

Character

In a letter to his trusted friend Andrew Jackson, Sam Houston wrote, "I would give no thought to what the world might say of me, if I could only transmit to posterity the reputation of an honest man."

For citizens of the Old South, character was everything. A person's good name was his most valued possession. Observe the following counsel, and you too can earn a reputation for honesty that would make old Sam Houston proud.

I cannot and will not cut my conscience
to fit this year's fashions.

Lillian Hellman

Honesty is the first chapter in
the book of wisdom.

Thomas Jefferson

Moral values never change.

Jimmy Carter

To Be Rather Than To Seem

State Motto of North Carolina

I leave this rule for others
when I'm dead.
Be always sure you're right—
then go ahead.

Davy Crockett

I cannot be intimidated from doing that which my judgment and conscience tell me is right by any power on earth.

Andrew Jackson

The one thing that doesn't abide by majority rule is a person's conscience.

Harper Lee

I would rather be right than President.

Henry Clay

Maintaining your integrity in a world of sham is no small accomplishment.

Wayne Oates

In matters of principle, stand like a rock;
    in matters of taste, swim with the current.

Thomas Jefferson

Let your tongue speak what your heart thinks.

Davy Crockett

When in doubt, tell the truth.

Mark Twain

For when the one Great Scorer comes
    to write against your name,
  He marks — not that you won or lost —
    but how you played the game.

Grantland Rice

Do your duty in all things. You cannot do more.
  You should never wish to do less.

Robert E. Lee

We must adjust to changing times and
  still hold to unchanging principles.

Jimmy Carter

Quoting his high school teacher, Julia Coleman

Follow truth wherever it may lead.

Thomas Jefferson

Character is power.

Booker T. Washington

Show class, have pride,
and display character.
If you do, winning
takes care of itself.

Bear Bryant

<u>10</u>

War

Southerners have never shied away from a fight. George Washington, a prominent Virginia planter, led troops in the Revolutionary War. Andrew Jackson, a North Carolinian by birth and a Tennessean by choice, led his army to victory in the Battle of New Orleans. Davy Crockett and Sam Houston, two transplanted Tennesseans, were key figures in the War of Texas Independence. Civil War heroes such as Stonewall Jackson are revered to this day.

The fate of unborn millions will now depend,
under God, on the courage and conduct
of this army.

George Washington

I have seen enough of one war
never to wish to see another.

Thomas Jefferson

The Union shall be preserved.

Andrew Jackson

Pop, pop, pop! Bom, bom, bom! Throughout the day — no time for memorandums now. Go ahead! Liberty and independence forever.

Col. Davy Crockett's last entry in his journal.

The Alamo, March 5, 1836

Remember the Alamo!

Battle Cry Of The Army Of Texas

There were no alternatives but victory or death.

Sam Houston

Describing the Texas Forces versus Santa Anna's Army

I know no South, no North, no East, no West
to which I owe my allegiance. The Union, sir,
is my country.

Henry Clay in 1848

United we stand, divided we fall.

State Motto of Kentucky

All we ask is to be left alone.

Jefferson Davis

From his inaugural address as
President of the Confederacy, 1861

I can anticipate no greater calamity for the
country than the dissolution of
the Union. I am willing to sacrifice
anything but honor for its preservation.
Robert E. Lee in 1861

If the Union is dissolved, and the government
disrupted, I shall return to my native state and
share the miseries of my people and, save in
defense, will draw my sword no more.
Robert E. Lee

It's a rich man's war and a poor man's fight.

Popular Description Of The Civil War

It is good that war is so terrible lest
  we should grow too fond of it.

Robert E. Lee

Spoken during the victory at the battle of Fredericksburg, 1862

Up, men, and to your posts! Don't forget
  today that you are sons of Old Virginia.

George Pickett

To his troops before their disastrous charge at the battle of
Gettysburg, 1863

This has been a sad day for us, a sad day;
  but we can't expect always to gain victories.

Robert E. Lee

Spoken after the defeat at Gettysburg

We have fought this fight as long and as well
as we know how. We have been defeated. For us,
as Christian people, there is now but one course
to pursue. We must accept the situation.

Robert E. Lee

Abandon your animosities and
make your sons Americans!

Robert E. Lee

Keep the memory of our heroes green.

Jefferson Davis

I'll never write my memoirs. I would be trading
on the blood of my men.

Robert E. Lee

I am the grandchild
of a lost war.

Katherine Anne Porter

In the moment of death,
the Confederacy entered
upon its immortality.

Robert Penn Warren

11

Work

In the Old South, unless you happened to own a large plantation, life was hard. The vast majority of Southerners, both black and white, struggled to scratch a living out of stubborn soil. There were no forty-hour work weeks in this agrarian society; the typical work day went from sunup to sundown. It's no wonder that Southerners have important things to say about hard work.

Work is the measure of worth.

W. C. Handy

Do for yourself or do without.

Gaylord Perry

I'm a great believer in luck, and I find
the harder I work, the more luck I have.

Thomas Jefferson

A substitute for hard work is worth about
one-tenth the real thing.

Grantland Rice

T. C. B.
Takin' Care of Business
Elvis Presley's Motto

Take time to deliberate; but when the time
for action arrives, stop thinking and go on.
Andrew Jackson

As long as you're doing something
interesting and good, you're in business.
Louis Armstrong

I've never had a job. I've always played baseball.
Satchel Paige

Take pleasure not in the score, but
in the game.

Bobby Jones

There is as much dignity in plowing a field
as in writing a poem.

Booker T. Washington

God does not ask your ability or inability.
He asks only your availability.

Mary Kay Ash

 P ractice, work hard, and give it
                       everything you have.

Dizzy Dean

 P laying in the big leagues wasn't
                  nearly as hard as getting there.

Hank Aaron

 T here are two kinds of talent, man-made talent
and God-given talent. With man-made talent you
have to work very hard. With God-given talent,
         you just touch it up once in a while.

Pearl Bailey

Don't apologize for your work.

Robert Penn Warren

Men expect too much, do too little.

Allen Tate

The hardest task is not to do what is right
but to know what is right.

Lyndon Baines Johnson.

Go out with a definite purpose and
stay with your work as long as
that purpose remains definite.

Bobby Jones

It is wonderful how much may be done
if we are always doing.

Thomas Jefferson

When we do the best we can, we never know
what miracles may result.

Helen Keller

Keep hammering away.

Hank Aaron

12

Southern Literature

Southern literature has a long and rich tradition. From Poe to Percy, from Faulkner to the Fugitives, Southerners inform and entertain. On the following pages, notable Southern writers explain their craft.

When a talk is made and put down, it is good to look at it afterward.

Sequoya

Tennessee-born Native American explaining why he invented
the Cherokee alphabet

It is the writer's privilege
to help man endure
by lifting his heart.

William Faulkner

The South and the West and other
faraway places have made and are making
American literature.

Katherine Anne Porter

Most Southern writers were produced by
a society in which people talk into the night
and tell stories.

Eudora Welty

Southerners talk music.

Mark Twain

Southern Wisdom

Southerners love a good tale. They are
born reciters, great memory retainers,
diary keepers, letter exchangers, letter savers,
history tracers and debaters, and —
outstaying all the rest — great talkers.

Eudora Welty

There are only two or three human stories,
and they go on repeating themselves
as fiercely as if they had never happened.

Willa Cather

First learn the laws of writing.
  Then rearrange them to suit yourself.
           Truman Capote

Writing is a craft. You have to take your
  apprenticeship in it like anything else.
          Katherine Anne Porter

Writing is the hardest work in the world,
  and one serves a longer apprenticeship
    than at any other trade.
          Margaret Mitchell

I spend three hours a day writing
  and the rest of the day getting over it.
          Flannery O'Connor

The writer's only responsibility is to his art.
William Faulkner

A good novel is possible only after
one has given up and let go.
Walker Percy

If I had to give young writers advice, I'd say
don't listen to writers talking about writing.
Lillian Hellman

The man who doesn't read good books has
no advantage over the man who can't read them.

Mark Twain

Literature is my Utopia.

Helen Keller

The writer wants to leave a scratch on the
wall of oblivion saying "Kilroy was here."

William Faulkner

13

Courage

Nobel Laureate and Mississippi native William Faulkner noted that "We must teach ourselves not to be afraid." Southerners have a long tradition of heroism, both in battle and at home. Although the giants of the past are gone, we still need heroes. Here are words of wisdom about one of the world's great renewable resources — courage.

Courage can achieve everything.

Sam Houston

Consult the spirit within you first.

Oprah Winfrey

Most people live and die with their music
still unplayed. They never dare to try.

Mary Kay Ash

Never take counsel of your fears.

Andrew Jackson

Become so wrapped up in something that you forget to be afraid.

Lady Bird Johnson

Courage is resistance to fear,
    mastery of fear — not absence of fear.

Mark Twain

Do not borrow trouble by dreading tomorrow.
    It is the dark menace of the future
      that makes cowards of us all.

Dorothy Dix

Everybody's afraid of himself.

Robert Penn Warren

Fear brings out the worst in everybody.

Maya Angelou

Never surrender your dreams.

Jesse Jackson

Be vigilant, be active, be brave.

Patrick Henry

Fear is an illusion.

Michael Jordan

One man with courage is a majority.

Andrew Jackson

14

Other People

There is a grand tradition known as "Southern hospitality." Southerners are renowned for their courteous treatment of others. But the truest form of hospitality goes beyond common courtesy. It is the ethical, compassionate treatment of others.

A life isn't significant except for its impact on other lives.

Jackie Robinson

Life is an exciting business and most exciting
when lived for others.

Helen Keller

These are two ways of exerting one's strength:
one is pushing down, the other is pulling up.

Booker T. Washington

There's no such thing as a self-made man.

Red Barber

People, you must remember, are
  awfully complex creatures, and you may be
  in for some surprises if you divide the cast
         into heroes and villains.

Robert Penn Warren

Herein lies the tragedy of the age: not that men
are poor — all men know something of poverty.
  Not that men are wicked — who is good?
  Not that men are ignorant — what is truth?
  No, the tragedy is that men know so little
         of other men.

W. E. B. Du Bois

Share an abiding respect for
         individual human rights.

Jimmy Carter

That old law about "an eye for an eye"
leaves everybody blind.
Martin Luther King, Jr.

Everybody comes from the same source.
If you hate another human being,
you're hating part of yourself.
Elvis Presley

Don't tell people what to do. The gifted
don't need it, and the others can't take it.
Katherine Anne Porter

There are some people who, if they don't know,
you can't tell 'em.
Louis Armstrong

Comparisons with other people are like weeds.
As soon as you deal with one, another one
pops up.

Hank Aaron

Don't bother just to be better than others.
Try to be better than yourself.

William Faulkner

Never give your power to another person.

Oprah Winfrey

Never desire a knowledge of
other peoples' business.

Dolly Madison

If anything goes bad, I did it. If anything goes
semi-good, we did it. If anything goes real good,
you did it. That's all it takes to get people
to win football games.

Bear Bryant

Sandwich every bit of criticism
between two heavy layers of praise.

Mary Kay Ash

Few things help an individual more than
for another to place responsibility upon him,
and to let him know that he is trusted.

Booker T. Washington

Thanks cost nothing.

Creole Saying

Where there is great love,
there are always miracles.

Willa Cather

You have to help your friends, or you won't have any.

Russell B. Long

15

The South

Colonel Harlan Sanders of fried chicken fame said, "I never met a Kentuckian who wasn't going home." The South is more than a region — it's a state of mind, and Southerners seem forever returning there.

Even if they've moved away, most people who
grew up in the South still consider
themselves Southern.

Lillian Hellman

God, as devout and devoted Southerners are
sure, took special pains in creating the South.

Jonathan Daniels

Southerners are, of course, a mythological
people . . . lost, by choice, in dreaming of
high days gone and big house burned;
now we cannot even wish to escape.

Jonathan Daniels

Southerners can never resist a losing cause.

Margaret Mitchell

In the South, the war is what A.D. is elsewhere;
they date from it.

Mark Twain

The South is a special case. It lost the war and
suffered hardship. That kind of defeat gives
the past great importance.

Robert Penn Warren

Too poor to paint and too proud to whitewash.

Description of Southern pride and poverty after the Civil War

The South? What does that mean? Look at
the difference between Atlanta and Birmingham,
between Covington, Louisiana, and
New Orleans, or between North and South
Louisiana. I sometimes think some parts of
the South are more like the North
than the North itself.

Walker Percy

A century since the Civil War is a long time.
The Confederate flag is often just confetti
in careless hands now.

Jonathan Daniels

Mississippi begins in the lobby
of a Memphis, Tennessee, hotel and
extends south to the Gulf of Mexico.

William Faulkner

All in all, Mississippi is a lush, pleasant place
to live, provided one enjoys the languor of a
subtropical climate, kindness, and a
relaxed atmosphere.

Pearl Bailey

If I ever get back to Georgia,
I'm gonna nail my feet
to the ground.

Lewis Grizzard

Alabama, for some reason I cannot explain,
seems to me to be the most Southern state
in the South.

Pearl Bailey

Appalachia is the only region of this country
with a real culture. It came to us from the
British Isles — the music, the dances, the
humor, the writers — but now it's ours,
and I think we'll keep it.

Jesse Stuart

One of those lovely mist mornings of late spring
when every flower in New Orleans seems to
melt and mix with the air.

Lillian Hellman

Butter melts faster in the South.

Roy Blount, Jr.

16

Observations On Death, Taxes, Rock and Roll, Mothers, and Other Inevitabilities Of Life

Porch-swing philosophy is a grand Southern tradition. We conclude with a potpourri of wisdom from Dixie.

He who knows most knows best how little he knows.

Thomas Jefferson

Fame is tough. When you're the top dog,
everybody wants to put you in the pound.

Charles Barkley

True happiness is not attained through
self-gratification but through fidelity
to a worthy purpose.

Helen Keller

Tradition is very often an excuse word
for people who don't want to change.

Red Barber

The urgent question of our time is whether we
can make change our friend, not our enemy.

Bill Clinton

Mountain-moving faith is not just dreaming
and desiring. It is daring to risk failure.

Mary Kay Ash

Hot heads and cold hearts never solved anything.

Billy Graham

The man who views the world at fifty
the same way he did at twenty has wasted
thirty years of his life.

Muhammad Ali

No one can figure out your worth but you.

Pearl Bailey

Elvis is dead, and I don't feel so good myself.

Lewis Grizzard

Death, taxes, and
childbirth! There's never
a convenient time
for any of them.

Margaret Mitchell

Have you called your momma today? I sure wish I could call mine.

Bear Bryant

Spoken on a television commercial

People generally see what they look for and
hear what they listen for.

Harper Lee

Dreams, if they're any good, are always
a little crazy.

Ray Charles

A flaw in a diamond stands out
while the blemish on a pebble is unnoticed.

Rebekah Baines Johnson

In a letter to her son, Lyndon Baines Johnson

There is time for departure even when
there is no certain place to go.

Tennessee Williams

The Good Lord can make you anything
you want to be, but you have to put
everything in His hands.

Mahalia Jackson

Consciously cultivate the ordinary.

Walker Percy

Arrogance has its own built-in misery.

Billy Graham

It ain't braggin' if you can do it.

Dizzy Dean

Every father who ever lived has
a dream for his son.

Grantland Rice

Church is a verb.

Will D. Campbell

Rock and roll is basically just gospel music
mixed with rhythm and blues.

Elvis Presley

Expect things of yourself.

Michael Jordan

I don't like money, actually,
but it quiets the nerves.

Joe Louis

If I had my life to live over, I'd make
the same mistakes, only sooner.

Tallulah Bankhead

Surely the consolation prize of old age is
finding out how few things are
worth worrying over.

Dorothy Dix

Don't look back.
Something might be
gaining on you.

Satchel Paige

Sources

Hank Aaron: (b. 1934) Home Run King, Baseball
   Executive, Alabama Native, Georgia Resident 16, 100,
   102, 124

James Agee: (1909-1955) Writer, Tennessean 30, 36

Muhammad Ali: (b. 1942) Boxing Icon, Louisville Native
   34, 48, 141

Louis Armstrong: (1898-1971) New Orleans Jazz Legend
   98, 123

Maya Angelou: (b. 1928) Poet, Author, Arkansas Native
   116

Mary Kay Ash: (B. 1915) Founder of Dallas-based Mary
   Kay Cosmetics 14, 18, 99, 113, 125, 139

Arthur Ashe, Jr.: (1943-1993) Tennis Player, Author,
   Native of Richmond, Virginia 37, 48

Pearl Bailey: (1918-1990) Virginia-born Entertainer 11, 22,
   48, 65, 100, 134, 136, 141

Tallulah Bankhead: (1903-1968) Actress, Alabama
   Native 147

Red Barber: (1908-1992) Sports Announcer, Born in
   Mississippi, Long-time Resident of Florida 121, 139

Charles Barkley: (b. 1963) Basketball Star, Alabama
   Native 139

Roy Blount, Jr.: (b. 1941) Writer, Humorist 136

Paul "Bear" Bryant: (1913-1983) Football Coach 40, 47,
   83, 125, 143

Archie Campbell: (1914-1987) Comedian, Television
   Personality, Tennessean 58

Will D. Campbell: (b. 1924) Author, Clergyman, Social
   Activist, Resident of Mount Juliet, Tennessee 68, 146

Truman Capote: (1924-1984) New Orleans-born Writer
   108

Jimmy Carter: (b. 1924) Governor of Georgia, U. S.
   President 78, 82, 122

Tennessee Ernie Ford: (1919-1991) Entertainer,
Tennessee Native 45, 52

Dizzy Gillespie (b. 1917) Jazz Musician, South Carolina
Native 23

Billy Graham: (b 1918): Clergyman, Evangelist, North
Carolinian 20, 34, 140, 146

Lewis Grizzard: (1946-1994) Writer, Humorist, Georgian
135, 141

W. C. Handy: (1873-1958) Alabama-born Musician,
Memphian, "Father of the Blues" 34, 36, 96

Lillian Hellman: (1905-1984) Playwright, Author 9, 19, 54,
78, 109, 130, 136

Patrick Henry: (1736-1799) Virginia Politician,
Revolutionary War Hero 60, 117

Sam Houston: (1793-1863) Lawyer, Soldier, Governor of
Tennessee, President of Texas 21, 77, 87, 112

Cordell Hull: (1871-1955) Statesman, Tennessean 73, 76

Andrew Jackson: (1767-1845) Tennessee Congressman,
U. S. Senator, General, U. S. President 70, 72, 74, 80, 86,
98, 114, 118

Jesse Jackson: (b. 1941) South Carolina Native, Civil
Rights Leader, Clergyman 28, 117

Mahalia Jackson: (1911-1972) Gospel Singer, Louisiana
Native 144

Thomas Jefferson: (1743-1826) Virginian, U. S. President,
Author, Architect, Founder of The University of Virginia
9, 15, 17, 32, 54, 57, 66, 70, 74, 78, 81, 82, 86, 96, 102, 138

Andrew Johnson: (1808-1875) Tennessee Senator, U. S.
President 74

Lyndon Baines Johnson: (1908-1973) Texan,
Congressman, Senator, President 26, 37, 49, 71, 72, 101

Lady Bird Johnson: (b. 1912) First Lady 71, 115

Rebekah Baines Johnson: Mother of Lyndon Baines
Johnson 144

Flannery O'Connor: (1925-1964) Writer, Georgia Native
27, 108

Jesse Owens: (1913-1980) Track Star, Olympic Champion, Alabama Native 18

Satchel Paige: (1906-1982) Baseball Player, Native of Mobile, Alabama 9, 20, 98, 148

Dolly Parton: (b. 1946) Entertainer, Entrepreneur, Tennessean 36

Claude Pepper: (1900-1989) Florida Congressman 73

Walker Percy: (1916-1990) Alabama-born Novelist, Louisiana Resident 40, 109, 133, 145

Gaylord Perry: (b. 1938) Baseball Player, Born in Williamston, North Carolina 96

George Pickett: (1825-1875) Confederate General 91

Elvis Presley: (1935-1977): Mississippi-born Memphis Native, Singer, Actor, Cultural Icon 8, 18, 97, 123, 146

Edgar Allan Poe: (1809-1849) Writer, Resident of Richmond, Virginia, Student at the University of Virginia 65

James K. Polk: (1795-1849) Tennessee Congressman and Governor, U. S. President, Born in North Carolina 70

Katherine Anne Porter: Texas-born Writer (1890-1980)
7, 22, 41, 93, 106, 108, 123

Grantland Rice: (1880-1954) Sportswriter, Tennessean
29, 35, 45, 64, 82, 96, 146

Jackie Robinson: (1912-1972) Pioneering Baseball Player, Born in Cairo, Georgia 120

James Robertson: (1742-1814) Explorer, Pioneer, "The Father of Middle Tennessee, " North Carolina Native 46

Sequoya: (1760-1843) Cherokee Chief 104

About the Author

Criswell Freeman is a Doctor of Clinical Psychology living in Nashville, Tennessee. He is the author of *When Life Throws You a Curveball, Hit It* and other books from WALNUT GROVE PRESS. He is also a published country music songwriter.

About Wisdom Books

Wisdom Books chronicle memorable quotations in an easy-to-read style. Written by Criswell Freeman, this series provides inspiring, thoughtful and humorous messages from entertainers, athletes, scientists, politicians, clerics, writers and renegades. Each title focuses on a particular region or special interest.

Combining his passion for quotations with extensive training in psychology, Dr. Freeman revisits timeless themes such as perseverance, courage, love, forgiveness and faith.

"Quotations help us remember the simple yet profound truths that give life perspective and meaning," notes Freeman. "When it comes to life's most important lessons, we can all use gentle reminders."